WORLD BANK WORKING PAPER NO. 121

Setting Standards for Communication and Governance

The Example of Infrastructure Projects

Lawrence J.M. Haas
Leonardo Mazzei
Donal O' Leary

THE WORLD BANK
Washington, D.C.

Copyright © 2007
The International Bank for Reconstruction and Development/The World Bank
1818 H Street, N.W.
Washington, D.C. 20433, U.S.A.
All rights reserved
Manufactured in the United States of America
First Printing: June 2007

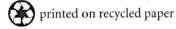 printed on recycled paper

1 2 3 4 5 10 09 08 07

ISBN-10: 0-8213-7169-X   ISBN-13: 978-0-8213-7169-5
eISBN: 978-0-8213-7170-1
ISSN: 1726-5878   DOI: 10.1596/978-0-8213-7169-5

Lawrence J.M. Haas is an Independent Consultant. Leonardo Mazzei a Communications Officer in the Development Communication division of the External Affairs department of the World Bank. Donal O' Leary is Senior Advisor at Transparency International in Berlin.

Library of Congress Cataloging-in-Publication Data has been requested.

Contents

Acknowledgments v

About the Authors vii

Acronyms ix

Foreword xi

Abstract xiii

1. Governance and Infrastructure Context 1

2. The Nature of Corruption Risks in Infrastructure Projects 7
   Corruption Risk—The Supply and Demand Perspective 7
   Corruption Vulnerability—The Project Cycle Perspective 8
   Pervasive Effects of Corruption in Infrastructure. 9
   Tools and Remedies for Corruption 9

3. Emerging Good Practice 13
   What Broader Observations May Be Drawn? 13

4. The Way Forward: Enhancing the Role of Communication to Foster Good
   Governance in Infrastructure Development. 17
   Building on Current Experience. 18
   Building on Current Experience and New Initiatives 19
   New Initiatives on Setting Standards—Guidance *and* Pressures 20

Appendix A: A Growing Body of Evidence 27

Appendix B: Case Studies. 33

References 47

LIST OF TABLES

1. Illustrative Case Studies Linking Governance and Communications 14
2. Illustrative Opportunities Map 19
3. Global and Regional Mainstream Concerns in Infrastructure Development where
   Development Communication Can Add Value 24

LIST OF FIGURES

1. Stakeholders in the Public Sector Governance System for Infrastructure 3
2. Corruption Vulnerabilities in Infrastructure Planning and Implementation 8
3. Public Promotion for the National Road Rehabilitation Project, Paraguay 35
4. Signing Ceremony for a Road Social Contract *(contrato social via)* in Paraguay . . . 36
5. View of the Morning Glory Spillway of the Bumbuna Hydroelectric Project, Sierra Leone 37
6. Launch of Radio Numbara FM 102.5 at Bumbuna Village, Sierra Leone 39
7. Radio Numbara FM 102.5 "on air" (Sierra Leone) 40
8. Construction of the Berg Water Supply Dam (Photo Courtesy of Water Wheel) 41
9. A Workshop to Assess Children's Perceptions of the Berg Water Project (Photo Courtesy of Siobhan McCarthy) 42
10. Location of the El Cajon Hydroelectric 44
11. A Photograph of the Dam and the Powerhouse, Mexico 45

LIST OF BOXES

1. Early Lessons from Rome 2
2. Where Does Communication Fit into Governance? 10
3. Integrity Pacts for Public Contracting 11
4. Communication Strategies 18
5. Communication Can Give Hard Evidence to Reinforce Political Support When it Counts 28
6. Communication Can Leverage Large Financial Returns through Accountability . . . 29
7. Communication Reinforces Transparency in Public Institutions 30
8. Communication Facilitates Processes of Social Change and Reform 30
9. Communication May Encompass Capacity Building for Media Roles in Infrastructure 31

Acknowledgments

The authors would like to thank the Government of Italy for their sponsorship of the first World Congress on Communication for Development (Rome, October 2006), which made this initiative possible.

In addition, the authors would like to acknowledge the support of the following individuals in the preparation of this paper:

- The Hon, Paa Kwesi Nduom, Minister of Public Sector Reform, Government of Ghana, for his excellent chairmanship of the session on "Setting Standards for Communication and Governance: The Example of Infrastructure Projects" at the World Congress on Communication for Development held in Rome, October 2006, where this paper was first presented.
- Mr. Andres G. Pizarro of the World Bank, who made available the photographs of the Paraguay National Road Maintenance Project.
- Mr. Mustapha Kargbo of the Project Implementation Unit (PIU), who made available the photographs of the Sierra Leone 50 MW Bumbuna Hydroelectric Completion Project.
- Lani van Vuuren, Public Understanding of Science Officer, Water Research Commission, South Africa, and Siobhan McCarthy, Communications Officer with Trans-Caledon Tunnel Authority, South Africa, both of whom made available the photos of the Berg Municipal Water Supply Project for Cape Town.

About the Authors

From 1980–1998, **Lawrence J.M. Haas** led multidisciplinary teams working with water and energy utilities and Commissions in Africa and Asia, both implementing projects and capacity building. From 1998–2000 he was a Team Leader in the Secretariat of the World Commission on Dams. Currently Mr. Haas is working in an independent capacity for organizations such as the IUCN, the World Bank and ADB helping to introduce sustainable practices into sector policy frameworks and projects being developed.

Leonardo Mazzei is an international expert in the use of strategic communication to assist governments on difficult reform programs and high risk projects. As a Communications Officer in the Development Communication Division of the World Bank, Mr. Mazzei has worked in several development initiatives in Africa, Central Asia and Central America with a focus on governance, infrastructure and private public partnerships in the energy and water sector. He has extensive experience in political risk analysis, public consultations processes, conflict resolution and opinion research.

From 1982–2005, **Donal O'Leary** was a Senior Power Engineer with the World Bank, working primarily with the Energy and Water Groups for the South Asia and Africa Regions. During 1997–2002, he worked with Siemens AG under the World Bank Staff Exchange Program. In this context, he represented Siemens in the Industry Group associated with the World Commission on Dams (WCD). Dr. O'Leary is currently managing the Secretariat of the Water Integrity Network (WIN), which is being hosted by Transparency International.

Acronyms

BPCB	Business Principles for Countering Bribery
BPI	Bribe Payers' Index
CPI	Corruption Perception Index
DevComm	Development Communication Division at the Work Bank
GWP	Global Water Partnership
ICOLD	International Commission on Large Dams
IHA	International Hydropower Association
INT	World Bank's Department of Institutional Integrity
IP	Integrity Pact for Public Procurement
IUCN	The International Union for the Conservation of Nature
IWRM	Integrated Water Resource Management
MDG	Millennium Development Goal
MDB	Multilateral Development Bank
NIP	National Integrity Pact
PREM	Sustainable Development Network, Poverty Reduction and Economic Management
TI	Transparency International
WCD	World Commission on Dams
WCCD	World Congress on Communication for Development
BHP	Bumbuna Hydroelectric Project, Sierra Leone
BWP	Berg Water Supply Project, South Africa
CFE	Comisión Federal de Electricidad, México
CMC	Cape Metropolitan Council, South Africa
DWAF	Department of Water Affairs and Forestry, South Africa
EPS	Social Participation Framework, Paraguay
LGA	Local Government Act (2004), Sierra Leone
MOPC	Ministry of Public Works and Communications, Paraguay
NACSA	National Commission for Social Action, Sierra Leone
WSPD	Water Service Development Plan, South Africa

Foreword

Over the last decade, there has been a growing consensus on the central roles that both basic infrastructure and good governance play in economic development and poverty reduction. More recently, in recognition of the increased democratization of the development process and the need and demand for increased stakeholder participation in decision-making, this consensus has widened to acknowledge the critical role that communication can play in improving governance, making infrastructure development sustainable, and designing more effective anticorruption strategies.

In the context of governance reform and infrastructure development, the role of Transparency International (TI) has been crucial in recognizing the importance of governance in the development of sustainable projects and long-term strategies for combating corruption. TI's flagship report, *The Global Corruption Report 2005,* had a special focus on corruption in construction and post-conflict reconstruction. A major emphasis of TI's activities has been in developing effective tools to combat corruption at the project level, which is particularly relevant for large infrastructure projects.

The World Bank plays a leading role in mobilizing financial support for the infrastructure sector, and also in guaranteeing that the infrastructure projects it finances comply with strict environmental and social policies and safeguards. In recent years the Bank has increasingly focused on the importance of good governance for sustainable development and the infrastructure sector emerges as a particularly relevant focus area. In this context, the Bank has increasingly highlighted the role that communication can play in designing and implementing sustainable infrastructure projects. It has been championing the use of communication programs from the early stages of project design to ensure the inclusion of relevant stakeholders in decision-making but also to guarantee the transparency of the development process.

More recently, the Bank has focused on governance issues. This paper responds directly to the discussion paper, "Strengthening World Bank Group Engagement on Governance and Anticorruption", in relation to which the Bank's Development Committee in March 2007 called for strengthening communication in all stages of the infrastructure project cycle.

We are pleased to note that this paper is a result of extensive collaboration among Bank and TI staff in pooling their expertise and knowledge in the areas of infrastructure, governance, and communication. It was first presented at the World Congress on Communication for Development, held in Rome on October 25–27, 2006 under the co-sponsorship of the World Bank and at which TI and the Bank organized a thematic session on "Good Governance in Practice: The Example of Infrastructure Projects."

Viewed though the lens of the communication sector, this paper covers a wide range of infrastructure projects, including water supply and sanitation, hydropower and roads. It draws on experiences from a spectrum of countries, ranging from Mexico and Paraguay to Sierra Leone and South Africa. These experiences have been distilled into proposed standards for good practice in the preparation and implementation of infrastructure projects by World Bank staff. These standards could also be used by other stakeholders, including governments, the private sector, civil society, the communications media, and donors/financiers in the preparation, implementation and monitoring of infrastructure projects.

We trust that this paper will contribute to the design of high-quality, cost-effective, and sustainable infrastructure projects, including facilitating the promotion of inclusive communication processes and effective anticorruption plans. We would encourage all stakeholders to read it and apply the relevant lessons to guide their involvement in infrastructure projects.

Dr. Cobus de Swardt
Managing Director
Transparency International, Berlin

Abstract

This paper outlines a number of practical initiatives to strengthen the role of development communication in infrastructure projects. The authors aim to facilitate better quality projects and to build consensus on the type of governance reforms needed to fight corruption, drawing on the experience of development agencies like the World Bank and Transparency International, the leading anticorruption NGO.

Fighting corruption is synonymous with improving governance through transparency, accountability and integrity. The paper starts by characterizing corruption vulnerabilities in infrastructure and proceeds to illustrate where communication has added value on a number of recent projects, both in respect to making the projects more sustainable and by incorporating anti-corruption measures into the project preparation and implementation phases. It draws on examples of mainly World Bank supported projects from the road, transport, power and water sectors in different governance contexts.

Five standard-setting initiatives are then outlined, which focus on promoting best practice (and the eventual development of operationally effective standards) to better integrate development communication into the project cycle of World Bank-supported infrastructure projects.

Part of the intellectual challenge in mainstreaming development communication in the case of infrastructure is to bridge the infrastructure and communication paradigms. While progress has been made over the past decade, this requires more emphasis on developing standards with collaboration by practitioners from both fields and a policy dynamic that guides and pressures the adoption of standards.

The paper suggests that today, from the perspective of the infrastructure practitioner and the development practitioner in general, development communication is at the same crossroads as environmentally sustainable development was in the early 1990's—but in a new context and perhaps with more urgent drivers for mainstreaming.

CHAPTER 1

Governance and Infrastructure Context

Development communication is a primary, but as yet underutilized, instrument to enhance sustainable infrastructure and to facilitate good governance in the fight against corruption.

Good governance is widely seen as a prerequisite for sustainable development, especially in countries where infrastructure plays a central role in the development agenda. Today many regions of the world where the pace of governance reform is most rapid are also the societies in which there are the greatest needs to invest in basic infrastructure and service delivery to sustain growth, poverty reduction and achievement of the millennium development goals (MDGs).

In low-income countries, current estimates of the financing needs for infrastructure development and management stand at about 7 percent of GDP and range as high as 9 percent of GDP.[1] Yet, it is not just the need to mobilize and utilize effectively the exceptionally large sums of investment that underlies the desire for improved governance around infrastructure. A combination of factors contributes to this need, such as the ability to unlock both public and private investment, to improve the quality and sustainability of infrastructure services, to instill confidence in public expenditures and to ensure the equitable distribution of costs and benefits of infrastructure development within society.

Good governance is a comparatively new field, relative to other development topics. The economic changes that have gathered pace globally since the late 1980's and 1990's require a new balance among government responsibility, public investment and the private

---

1. World Bank website on infrastructure financing topics http://web.worldbank.org/WBSITE/ EXTERNAL/EXTABOUTUS/ORGANIZATION/EXTINFNETWORK/0,,contentMDK:20535656~menu PK:1827891~pagePK:64159605~piPK:64157667~theSitePK:489890,00.html

---

Box 1: Early Lessons from Rome

In a state where corruption abounds, laws must be very numerous.
– Publius Cornelius Tacitus, Roman historian, circa AD 56–177.

---

sector, whereby government plays a more enabling and regulating role. Lowering the walls between public and private investment also embodies a shift in the rights and responsibilities of all players in government, civil society and private sectors. At the same time, awareness of the urgency to fight corruption has grown, not only with greater openness but also with the proliferation of rent-seeking opportunities.

The quote from the Roman Empire in Box 1 illustrates that corruption risk in public investment has long been recognized.[2] It reinforces the notion that dealing with entrenched corruption needs long-term strategies with mechanisms that are an integral part of sustainable infrastructure development applied in culturally specific ways. There is a growing awareness of the important role that civil society, the media and the voluntary sector can play in promoting good governance and in democratizing development processes. Development communication can offer both a theoretical foundation and methodological approaches to support the necessary social and institutional transformations. Bringing the infrastructure and communication paradigms together will assist with the challenge of moving infrastructure programs forward.

The use of communication as a primary instrument to enhance sustainable infrastructure and to facilitate good governance subscribes to the broader theory that communication for development is "a social process, designed to seek a common understanding among all the participants of a development initiative, creating a basis for concerted action."[3] Enhancing development communication strengthens the foundations for good governance by promoting more open government, increased accountability and the active engagement of participants in civil society (World Bank 2005). It accepts the view that combating corruption is synonymous with improving governance around infrastructure.

Public opinion research shows that corruption is among the top governance concerns of people and leaders around the world, and it is central to national and international development dialogues on infrastructure. As the World Bank President remarked in an often-quoted statement at a conference in Indonesia in 2006:

> Today one of the biggest threats to development in many countries is corruption. It weakens fundamental systems, it distorts markets, and it encourages people to apply their skills and energies in non-productive ways. In the end governments and citizens will pay a price, a price in lower incomes [and] lower investment . . .
>
> —President Paul Wolfowitz, Jakarta speech, April 11, 2006

---

2. "The Many Faces of Corruption: Tackling vulnerabilities at the sector level," edited by Edgardo Campos and Sanjay Pradhan. The completed volume is planned for release in May 2007. Also see article in the anti-corruption newsletter at the following website. http://newsletters.worldbank.org/external/default/main?menuPK=583418&theSitePK=583411&pagePK=64133601&contentMDK=21030836&piPK=64129599

3. A definition of development communication advanced in the draft version of the paper, "Mainstreaming Communication For Development," Jan Servaes (co-ordinator) et al., July draft, 2006.

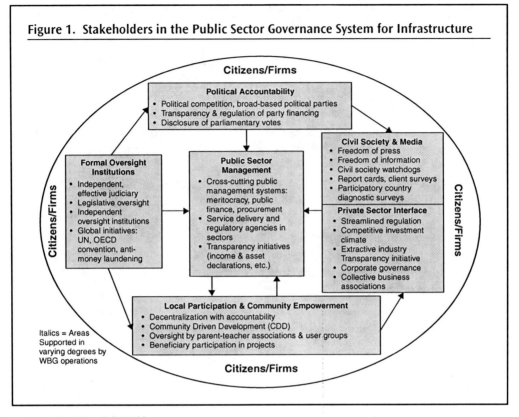

Figure 1. Stakeholders in the Public Sector Governance System for Infrastructure

Source: World Bank (2006b).

The broader framework linking reforms in governance to the fight against corruption in infrastructure has been outlined by the international community through the collaboration of donors, governments, international organizations and international civil society in many dialogue processes.

Figure 1 illustrates the range of actors broadly comprising the public sector governance system as presented in the discussion paper, "Strengthening Bank Group Engagement On Governance and Anticorruption." This paper was circulated to industry and civil society representatives like Transparency International (TI) for comment prior to its presentation at a meeting of the World Bank's high-level Development Committee.[4]

Reactions to the paper show the degree of consensus at the international level on the urgency, entry points and shared responsibility for governance reform around infrastructure. It includes an explicit call to expand the role of development communication. As noted in Figure 1, the main actors in the call to action include: (a) the central government executive, including cross-cutting control agencies responsible for public finance and

---

4. World Bank (2006b). Civil society and private sector feedback on the draft paper on Strengthening Bank Group Engagement On Governance and Anticorruption is also included on the same website. http://www.worldbank.org/governancefeedback

human resource management, and front-line regulatory and service provision agencies; (b) formal oversight institutions outside the executive, including the judiciary, parliament and other independent oversight institutions; (c) sub-national governments and local communities, with their own service provision responsibilities, and often their own local arrangements for control and accountability; (d) civil society and the private sector, both in their role as watchdogs (including the independent media) and as the 'recipients' of services and regulations, and hence a potential source of pressure for better performance; and (e) political actors and institutions at the apex, setting the broad goals and direction.

An effective communication strategy is clearly central to bring the actors together, whether work occurs at the national, sector or project level.

Communication provides a crucial analytical device and an important management tool to promote sustainable infrastructure development in three primary respects:

1. *Improve the quality of infrastructure:* Enable more inclusive and informed decision-making at all stages of the project cycle, driving new thinking and innovation to create sustainable infrastructure and to establish consensus on service provision priorities, where:

   ■ Informed decisions need effective communication strategies for engagement of multiple government agencies, civil society, private sector interests and the beneficiaries;

   ■ Innovation emerges from open dialogue processes, which allow a voice for all stakeholders and build consensus on balancing competing needs for service provision; and

   ■ Communication strategies provide key messages and mechanisms for timely information access and exchange, dialogue, conflict resolution and media participation essential to mobilize public input and support for project decisions.

2. *Build consensus on governance reforms around infrastructure:* Raise awareness of corruption vulnerabilities at all stages of infrastructure development and establish consensus on reform programs, including the partnerships and tariffs needed to make services sustainable, where:

   ■ Lack of awareness of the scale and effects of corruption or tools to fight corruption inhibit political will to combat corruption;

   ■ Wider consensus building is needed on practical details of governance reform, new behaviors and roles expected, and implications for infrastructure service provision—as hastily implemented and poorly supported reforms can be counterproductive;

   ■ Partnership approaches (e.g., public-private and community partnerships with the private sector) rely on structured processes for information sharing, dialogue and negotiation central to partnership formation and success; and

   ■ Media support and public communication is necessary to build consensus on the tariffs reforms needed to sustain or scale-up infrastructure services.

3. *Concerted action to manage corruption risks on infrastructure:* Maintain pressure for implementing reforms and build consensus on concrete measures to deal with corruption and to mainstream these actions, where:

- Tackling corruption is in the interests of all stakeholders involved with, or affected by, infrastructure projects, including the voluntary and involuntary risk takers;[5]
- Tackling corruption is a gradual, long-term process that involves changing attitudes that tolerate corrupt practices, re-training staff and restructuring institutions; and
- Concerted action requires prioritizing methods for achieving transparency, engagement of civil society and mechanisms for regular monitoring and gathering feedback to enlist the support of all stakeholders.

---

5. Discussion advanced in the World Commission on Dams Report (2000) http://dams.org, where risks refer to the risks of all stakeholders in hydropower project development. The notion of risk extends beyond traditional engineering, financial and economic risk (e.g., voluntary risks taken by governments, developers, dam owners/operators and financiers), to involuntary risk absorbed by people affected by a project and the environment as a public good. As stakeholders in a hydropower development, project-affected communities face risks to their rights as well as their resource access, livelihoods and welfare that need to be minimized. Their risk exposures also need to be managed—similar to risk management for voluntary risk takers. The notion of risk in this application is further advanced in the paper "Rights, Risks and Responsibilities—Scoping Report: An approach to implementing stakeholder participation," prepared for the IUCN, 2005. http://www.virtualcentre.org/ru/dec/toolbox/Refer/PRAl.htm

CHAPTER 2

The Nature of Corruption Risk in Infrastructure Projects

Transparency International's (TI) definition of corruption—the misuse of entrusted power for private gain—is widely cited and encompasses most other definitions (Stalgren 2006). The ability of the infrastructure sector to generate large rents and to provide vital services that are highly prized and highly political creates a fertile breeding ground for corruption (World Bank 2006b). Corruption vulnerabilities or risks in infrastructure projects can be categorized to locate the entry points and to demonstrate the role that communication can play in minimizing corruption risks.

Corruption Risk—The Supply and Demand Perspective

While the causes and impacts of corruption vary from country to country, corruption in infrastructure is sometimes characterized as supply and demand driven. Supply represents the behavior of "the payer" or "the supplier" and the reasons for his behavior. Demand describes the behavior of "the taker" or "the demander" and the reasons for his behavior. Either side can initiate a corrupt act.[6]

The supply side thus encompasses the domestic private sector involved in infrastructure, as well as international actors. TI's Bribe Payers' Index (BPI) ranks the propensity of private enterprises in particular countries to pay bribes. Instruments such

---

6. A Survey of Corruption Issues in the Mining and Mineral Sector, IIED 2001, Ian E. Marshall, supported but the World Business Council for Sustainable development available at http://ww1.transparency.org/working_papers/mining_mineral/survey_of_corruption_marshall.pdf#search=%22Survey%20of%20Corruption%20Issues%20in%20the%20Mining%20and%20Mineral%20Sector%22

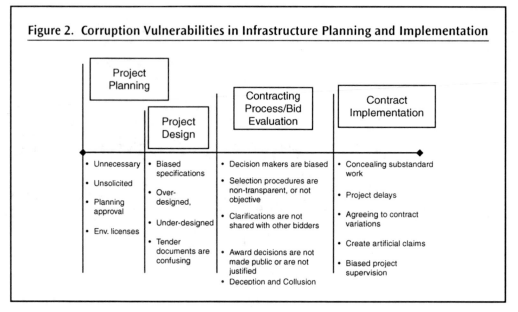

Figure 2. Corruption Vulnerabilities in Infrastructure Planning and Implementation

Source: O'Leary (2006).

as the OECD Convention on Combating Bribery of Foreign Public Officials are aimed at the international actors, though TI criticizes the OECD Convention follow-up with apparent limited enforcement in at least two thirds of OECD countries since it came into force in 1999.[7] TI's Corruption Perception Index (CPI) documents a country's reputation for honest practice, and countries with an adverse rating can be perceived as high on demand-side corruption.

Corruption Vulnerability—The Project Cycle Perspective

Figure 2 illustrates the range of corruption vulnerabilities for infrastructure projects to address in the planning and implementation phases of the project cycle. These vulnerabilities start in strategic planning and project selection with the potential for undue political influence in the selection of projects or inter-departmental collusion in project approval. Perhaps the most significant category of corruption is grand corruption in the form of bid rigging and kickbacks associated with the public procurement process or in the corruption of contract administration and supervision (for exmaple, kickbacks to accept inflated bills unit costs and amounts of material).

Vulnerabilities also continue during the project operation and maintenance phases. In some countries there is endemic petty corruption related to service access and provision, misappropriation or misuse of project revenues or unabashed use of "Official-Owned"

7. TI, "Enforcement of the OECD Anti-Bribery Convention is still deficient despite progress: New Report," 2006, at http://www.transparency.ca/Reports/20060724%20-%20TI%20OECD%20Second%20Report%20Press%20Release.pdf

enterprises. Another form of corruption is the failure to honor commitments for ongoing social and environmental mitigation management that adversely impacts the affected communities during project operation. The cycle of corruption depicted in Figure 2 can start all over again with procurement for maintenance, refurbishment and infrastructure upgrading contracts.

Pervasive Effects of Corruption in Infrastructure

The economic costs of corruption in infrastructure development and service provision are staggering. The African Union estimates that about one quarter (US$148 billion) of Africa's gross domestic product is "lost to corruption each year."[8] TI estimates that globally at least US$400 billion per year is lost to bribery and corruption in public procurement, increasing government costs by about 20–25 percent.

The effects of such losses on infrastructure strategies of countries are manifest. These include, for example, higher project costs and charges for infrastructure services and longer timeframes for provision of infrastructure services, which has a disproportionate impact on the poor and vulnerable most in need of services. Corruption is thus seen as a major cause of poverty as well as a barrier to overcoming it. Corruption can also sacrifice environmental sustainability and the ecosystem services on which many people rely for livelihoods, such as bribes paid to allow for excessive extraction from rivers and ground water reservoirs or pollution releases into water bodies.

It is generally accepted that chronic corruption undermines the political sustainability of infrastructure development, leads to conflict and deters investors and financiers concerned about their reputational risk, among other costs (World Bank 2006b). In infrastructure, the cumulative impacts of "petty" corruption can be devastating to the operation of power and water utilities.

Tools and Remedies for Corruption

TI's work is illustrative of the role of civil society and the nature of the tools and remedies that need communication processes for support and effectiveness.

Three tools are referenced to here:

- ▇ National Integrity Pacts (NIPs),
- ▇ Business Principles for Countering Bribery (BPCB), and
- ▇ Integrity Pacts for Public Procurement (IPs).

The NIP approach takes as its starting point the notion of "Institutional Pillars of Integrity" whereby a society becomes resistant to corruption when a whole series of

---

8. TI Internal Draft Paper, Corruption In Public Procurement: A Perennial Challenge, Glenn Ware et al, June 2006, citing the original source as Thachuk, K. (Winter-Spring 2005). "Corruption and International Security" SAIS Review, Vol. XXV, No. 1: 143152. Page 149.

Box 2: Where Does Communication Fit into Governance?

Communication is the basis of Transparency, which is the basis of Accountability, which in turn is the basis of Integrity.

Transparency International in Latin America and the Caribbean (TILAC) is the network of TI's 14 national chapters (NCs) in the region. One factor that was and continues to be crucial in the positioning of the TILAC network through the impact of its work is the focus on communications.

In 2001 TILAC and the Americas department designed a regional communications programme with the aim to "inform, mobilise and involve different audiences on anti-corruption matters by effectively relating to them through a wide range of communication vehicles."

Beyond developing a common TILAC communication strategy and strengthening the NC's communication structures, the work included the participatory and professional production, adaptation and dissemination of relevant TI and TILAC messages. The Ford Foundation supported the communication programme from August 2002 to July 2004 in three substantive areas: capacity building, internal and external communications.

A strong pillar for future communications activities is the Communication's Network, comprised of NC communications point people. The investment in the communications capacities of the Chapters and the network has been particularly important in terms of TILAC's effectiveness.

---

institutions are present and functioning well. These include the institutions noted previously in Figure 1 (O'Leary 2006). TI developed the NIP as a systems approach in which organizations work together to develop good governance practices to fight corruption and to take mutually reinforcing steps in their own spheres of influence or "shops."

From the civil society perspective, a good deal of resources and time are devoted to the central themes of accountability and independent monitoring. Accountability is now being defined as "downward" and "upward." For example, MDGs may define upward responsibility to their Boards and downward responsibility to their clients and beneficiaries, including civil society. Civil society needs effective communication strategies to be successful in this role (as in Box 2). An effective project communication strategy must inform beneficiaries sufficiently to monitor the delivery of project benefits and to define the roles of civil society roles clearly. Feedback links should enable the beneficiaries' voice on project performance and, where appropriate, on corrective actions. These communication mechanisms include not only "whistle blowing" but also report cards and hot lines.

From the industry or private sector perspective, it is equally important for infrastructure actors to work both with other stakeholders groups and with their own associations. TI has been working with industry to formulate a set of Business Principles for Countering Bribery (BPCB). A key message being promoted is that integrity and a level playing field are "good for business."

To illustrate one application of BPCB in infrastructure, in April 2006, the TI Chapter in Colombia facilitated the signature of a sectoral anti-bribery agreement among 11 water pipe manufacturers. Largely self-financed by the signatories to the agreement, it is estimated that the existence of this agreement is leading to a decrease in tender prices of approximately 30 percent. Nine water pipe manufacturers in Argentina signed a similar agreement in December 2005 (O'Leary 2006).

In the water sector, the newly formed Water Integrity Network (WIN) is advocating an approach based on the concepts of "PACTIV." The letters of the acronym represent five

---

Box 3: Integrity Pacts for Public Contracting

■ The *Process* includes an agreement between a government, government department or utility and all bidders for a public sector contract.

■ *Rights and Obligations*, are set out in the contract such that neither the government nor the contactors shall pay, offer, demand or accept bribes, or collude with competitors to obtain the contract during its execution. Bidders are required to disclose all commissions and similar expenses paid by them to anybody in connection with the project.

■ *Monitoring* is carried out by CSOs or independent private sector individuals or companies hired by the government, with the obligation to inform the public of any impropriety the contract parties are unwilling to correct. Alternatively, government can commit to full public disclosure of all relevant data regarding the evaluation of competing bids.

■ *Sanctions* apply when violations occur. For bidders they may range from loss or denial of contract, forfeiture of bid or performance bond and liability for damages, to blacklisting for future contracts. For government employees, criminal or disciplinary action.

---

vital building blocks for combating corruption in the water sector: Political leadership, Accountability, Capacity, Transparency, Implementation and Voice (Stalgren 2006).

Box 3 illustrates the main features of Integrity Pacts (IPs). For infrastructure projects, IPs should cover all activities from the selection of consultants for project feasibility and other preparatory studies, to the preparation of bidding documents and award of contract, right through to project implementation and handover to the client. One illustration is the IP agreement between the Karachi Water and Sewerage Board and Transparency International Pakistan on the award of contracts for the Pakistan Greater Karachi Water Supply Scheme.[9] As a result of a well-managed procurement process with an IP, the total cost of contracts awarded over 2002–2003 was 18.5 percent less than the cost estimate by the Government of Pakistan. Since 2003, approximately 57 IPs have been put in place worldwide: four in the water supply and sanitation sectors, five in the energy sector, ten in the telecommunications sector and eleven in the construction sector.

A wide array of other tools and remedies to fight corruption has been identified through the efforts of many international and national organizations. Conventions from institutions such as the United Nations (UN) and the United Nations Development Program (UNDP) back model legislation and legal instruments to reform national legislation.

---

9. O'Leary (2006). This refers to the Phase V, Stage II, 2nd 100 MGD, K III Project in Pakistan.

CHAPTER 3

Emerging Good Practice

The Appendixes contain a "body of evidence" to illustrate the role and value added by communication in infrastructure projects. Four case studies drawn from the road, water and power sectors are highlighted in Figure 2.

In Appendix A, these case studies are described under each of the five themes of the WCCD to illustrate the relevance of each theme to infrastructure challenges today.[10] In Appendix B, added value of communications to each project is discussed in relation to the country context.

What Broader Observations May Be Drawn?

The evidence in these case studies, as well as the larger body of experience, provide broad observations on the challenges in strengthening the role of communication to advance governance reform and sustainable infrastructure, including the following:

■ *Significant variations in approaches exist across infrastructures sectors:* Actions at the project level both influence and depend on governance reforms at the sector and

---

10. The presentation of the case studies in the Appendix are structured around the five themes of the WCCD, namely:
   i. Securing Political Will: The Prerequisite for Political Reform.
   ii. Strengthening Voice and Accountability: The Endgame of Communication for Development.
   iii. Making Public Institutions Transparent: The Cornerstone of an Open Society.
   iv. Fighting Corruption: Beyond Technocratic Solutions.
   v. Building Media Systems: Enabling an Effective Fourth Estate.

Table 1. Illustrative Case Studies Linking Governance and Communications

Case 1 Paraguay: The National Road Maintenance Project	Case 2 Sierra Leone: The 50 MW Completion of the Bumbuna Hydroelectric Project	Case 3 South Africa: The Berg Municipal Water Supply Project for Cape Town	Case 4 Mexico: The 750 MW El Cajon Hydropower Project
Demonstrates how anti-corruption elements were incorporated in the design of a national road improvement project. A Governance Improvement Plan and Road Social Contracts capture the measures stakeholders agreed upon for corruption prevention, deterrence and detection, and ensure public expenditures are more sustainably balanced between road expansion and road maintenance.	Demonstrates the effective integration of strategic communication in project preparation in a post-war setting. Conceives of communication to facilitate consensus in the distribution of the project benefits and enabling a grass-roots voice in developing the environment and social management components of the project, consistent with national governance reforms to promote local decision-making.	Demonstrates the importance of public communication capacity in agencies dealing with water supply infrastructure. Shows how a combination of legislative reform and new guidelines for consultation made institutions transparent. This strategy empowered public debate to reach a decision on water supply infrastructure for Cape Town and firmly placed demand-side management on the agenda.	Demonstrates the value of independent verification and review of contract bid and contractor selection processes for hydropower projects, together with increased civil society participation in monitoring the contract award process. Provides techniques suitable to scale-up across the power sector and replicate in public procurement processes in other infrastructure sectors.

country level. Moreover, "ring-fenced" projects that operate outside of the country's regular rules can weaken the overall project control environment and encourage patronage and corruption. Some donor-financed road sector projects have gone further than others in incorporating governance-related anti-corruption components explicitly into the early stages of project preparation. There is also evidence of interest in transferring successful experience across sectors in the same country. There is no informal or formal standard. To enlist expanded stakeholder cooperation or coalitions, it may be useful to explore the scope to introduce anti-corruption components in infrastructure projects in various sectors, such as power, and to broaden the discussion beyond procurement processes.

■ *Minimalist and strategic views of the role of communication compete:* Communication needs to be strategically as well as practically oriented on infrastructure projects. Effectively fighting corruption and encouraging sustainability requires engagement with institutions outside the central government, such as parliament, civil society, non-governmental organizations (NGOs), the media and local communities. Strategic communication tools are central to that effort. More typically, however, practitioners see the role of communication in a narrow or traditional way, one focused on dissemination. Actions in communication are still taken more often in response to a crisis than in a strategic effort to avert crises through the life of a project.

■ *Communications activities are typically under funded at all stages of the project cycle:* Evidence suggests a common weakness in many projects that experience difficulty is the lack of a coherent and effective communication strategy linking the needs, expectations and concerns of the different stakeholder interests to the project. Apart from controversy, symptoms of under funding communication functions include ad hoc approaches, lack of up-front communication and strategic planning. This observation applies equally to the budgets of ministries and agencies sponsoring infrastructure projects, as it does to the project preparation activities of donors. It is recognized that project managers must balance competing priorities for resources. To address this concern, standards on the role of communication should be applied at each stage of the project cycle. Another important line of argument to support resource allocation for communication is to link gains in corruption "savings" and to show a clear body of evidence on the financing gains from the transparency that is enabled by strategic communication.

■ *Bridging the infrastructure and communication paradigms is key to mainstreaming reform:* It is not difficult to see there is still a paradigm gap between infrastructure practitioners and communications practitioners. Part of the intellectual challenge is to bridge the two different paradigms, aided by collaborative development of standards. While donor teams are usually interdisciplinary, there are still issues to address in respect to the skills mix on project preparation teams, for example, to ensure that the communication functions are properly resourced. The challenge is perhaps more pronounced in developing countries, where sector agencies responsible for infrastructure projects have a long history of relative autonomy.

CHAPTER 4

The Way Forward: Enhancing the Role of Communication to Foster Good Governance in Infrastructure Development

The recent discussion paper, "Strengthening Bank Group Engagement On Governance and Anticorruption" cited previously offered a view of how communication standards can improve governance in infrastructure projects (World Bank 2006b). As a starting point, it postulates a basic standard may be to routinely prepare communication strategies for all phases of the project cycle, incorporating the elements as suggested in Box 4.

Civil society and industry reviewers agreed with these conclusions, but they had some suggestions to go further and faster. For example, TI urged the World Bank Group to "utilize its communication tools and global reach more extensively to strengthen public understanding regarding the damaging effects of corruption on sustainable development, economic growth, poverty reduction, environmental protection, the achievement of the Millennium Development Goals and critical issues of global security. It should widely and publicly disseminate the lessons learned from its own and others' work as well as publicize the Bank's commitment to address this issue vigorously."

What also emerged from the feedback was that more attention to public communication can help governments improve their capacity to build consensus to move forward with those elements of sector reform packages that are most difficult. Better communication strategies can assist with reform measures, such as introducing public-private partnerships for service provision, improving cost recovery, eliminating vandalism, improving customer service response times and promoting conservation and tariff reforms.

Standards for communication and governance must extend beyond general guidance, raising a set of practical questions, including what type of standards are needed, how prescriptive they should be if at all, and what urgency is there in moving beyond discretionary standards.

Box 4: Communication Strategies

"Because of the importance of an effective dialogue on issues of fraud and corruption, it is important to develop an effective communication strategy that covers all phases of the project. The communication plan must provide for consistent messages to be conveyed to all of the relevant stakeholders: government officials in the implementing agency; contractors, suppliers, and consultants who may be involved in bidding on the project; members of civil society affected by the project; and (as appropriate) the local press. The role of the media may be especially important if the plan includes the use of publicity—both positive and negative stories—as a tool for reducing the level of fraud and corruption in Bank projects. The objective would be to highlight both noteworthy achievements in quality, cost-effectiveness, and sustainability, as well as any incidents of alleged collusion, fraud, or corruption."

Source: World Bank (200b).

The literature provides some comparisons, in particular recalling the environmental impact assessments (EIAs) that were introduced in the 1980's for most infrastructure projects. At that time, some policy-makers and practitioners argued that the requirements and standards for EIAs would impair project progress, be too costly and retard development. Today environmental impact assessments are a fact of life in large public works projects. In many respects, therefore, development communication today is at the same crossroads that environmentally sustainable development was at that time, however, in a new context and perhaps with more urgent drivers.

Building on Current Experience

Over the past decade many practical steps have been taken by MDBs and others to promote generic standards to better integrate communication in infrastructure projects. By extension, these efforts aim to create wider awareness of what is needed to mainstream development communication.

The Development communication Division at the Work Bank (DevComm) has, for example, been actively building a sector-by-sector inventory of good practice case studies and tool kits to support operational staff. The recent publication, "The Role of Communication in Large Infrastructure" on the Bumbuna hydroelectric project in Sierra Leone (Case Study 2 in this paper) is an example of this work. DevComm materials provide practical guidance on what issues trigger the need for communication and consultations and they also outline the typical costs and timeline for integrating communication in the project cycle for both donor and client executed work. Another example of this work is DevComm's publication on water projects, "Communication for Water Reform: A Guide for Task Team Leaders."[11, 12]

---

11. For example, the major costs of the communications components for a water reform program in St. Lucia were for the local firm that did the public opinion research, and then designed and implemented the communication campaign. Total costs were US$100,000 over a 2-year period. Additional budget was required for the communication specialist in the utility (WASCO).

12. Communications budgets and issues for hydropower projects are discussed in the Bumbuna hydropower project report referred to earlier. For the project preparation phase of hydropower projects communications components can costs up to US$200,000 on larger project, or be scaled at roughly a quarter to a third of the cost of the EIA. Supervision time requirements are roughly equivalent to those for EIAs when power sector reforms are part of the project, otherwise less (authors' comment).

Building on Current Experience and New Initiatives

Casting the net more broadly, Table 2 illustrates a more comprehensive approach to integrating communication in infrastructure with reinforcing elements of: (1) shared knowledge development, (2) advocacy, (3) standard setting and (4) building coalitions, networks and partnerships. This partly illustrates the dynamic where steps already taken need further nurturing and new initiatives need to be introduced based on regularly taking stock with measurable progress indicators. Table 2 demonstrates opportunities to strengthen both governance

Table 2. Illustrative Opportunities Map

	Corruption and Governance Centered	Communication Facilitation
Knowledge development: Tools & Good Practice	– Expand good practice with different instruments at project and sector levels – Tailor and target tool kits to key actor groups (parliamentary committees and policy makers, project managers, etc.) – Develop and disseminate a broader repertoire of potential anticorruption measures and tools – Develop corruption risk analysis techniques to apply in project appraisals – Prepare "how to/what you need to know" papers for topics important for Advocacy (as in the next block)	– Expand the inventory of good practice with strategic communication in different infrastructure sectors and along the project cycle, targeting project managers – More comprehensive tool kits, or ones focused on infrastructure projects – Develop guidance for communications practitioners on what communications tools support new anti-corruption instruments (e.g., NIP, IP, Social Contracts, Corruption Risk Assessments) – Prepare "how to/what you need to know papers" for topics important in advocacy (as in the next block)
Advocacy Tools: Essays, Testimonials and Hard Evidence	– Hard Evidence: Research deepens knowledge of the sources of corruption – Hard Evidence: Value-added of anti-corruption through good practice, i.e., low hanging fruit and longer term – Analysis: What decision makers need to know about corruption in infrastructure projects – Analysis: The role of ethics as a part of institutional anti-corruption strategies – Analysis: How to expand integrity requirements to contractors and consultants as a condition for involvement in projects – Essay: Demand and supply side corruption in the infrastructure sector	– Hard Evidence: Good communication adds value to infrastructure ($ and sense) – Paradigm Bridging Analysis: looking at top concerns of infrastructure practitioners from communication practitioner's view – Analysis: What pitfalls a project manager needs to avoid in working with the media – Essays: Testimonials on communication in infrastructure projects from different perspectives: industry, civil society, the media, and governments

(Continued)

Table 2. Illustrative Opportunities Map (*Continued*)

	Corruption and Governance Centered	Communication Facilitation
Setting Standards: Towards Good Practice and Safeguards	Focusing on Projects Supported by MDBs and Donors: – Corruption risk assessments in project appraisals – Governance and anticorruption plans: as component of infrastructure projects, which could include the use of tools such as IPs and BPCB – Compliance plans: implementation and operation commitments – Anti-Corruption as a potential safeguard triggered by infrastructure projects	Focusing on Projects Supported by MDBs and Donors: – Communication instruments for different stages of the project cycle—minimum standards as seen from the perspective of project managers and stakeholders – Standards that embody the role of communication in operational policy (policy-by-policy where relevant) – Standards for communication participation and support on mission teams – Standards for communication capacity on client country project teams, project coordination units, etc. – Guidelines/standards for budgets for communication functions on donor supported projects
Building Coalitions, Networks and Partnerships	– Supporting the Water Integrity Network (WIN) – Working with networks like the Global Water Partnership (GWP) to introduce a corruption dimension in Integrated Water Resource Management (IWRM) – Expanding the use of Integrity Pacts (IP) in cooperation with industry associations – More civil society, industry and governance confidence building initiatives in transitional economies (e.g., central Europe)	– Linking development communication networks better with anti-corruption network (WCDD follow-up) – Linking development communication networks better to infrastructure networks and associations (e.g., technical committees of the International Commission on Large Dams (ICOLD) with Development communication groups) – Joint dissemination activities and collaboration in newsletters, etc.

and communication for infrastructure development with public international support. It does not address service provision dimensions or private sector-led projects.

New Initiatives on Setting Standards—Guidance *and* Pressures

It is helpful to look at standards for communication and governance from the perspective of creating a "supply and demand" balance, one that both guides and pressures the evolution and adoption of standards. Supply-side initiatives, if that term may be used, characterize current efforts to strengthen the distillation and adoption of good practice. Demand-side initiatives, on the other hand, aim to build consensus and create pressure for the eventual development of operationally effective standards, like the MDB operational and safeguard policies for donor-supported projects.

The authors' view is that formal standards to address corruption in infrastructure will eventually be on the agenda to help ensure consistency and quality in lending across all sectors. However, it is important to guarantee that such standards are ready, tested and practical—and will receive support not only in stakeholder discussions but also in the field.

The following five initiatives are proposed to move thinking about communication standards for infrastructure forward on a number of fronts.

Initiative 1: Instruments to Apply in the Project Cycle—The Necessary Tools

The first initiative responds to the Development Committee call to prepare effective communication strategies for projects, covering all phases of the project cycle (as noted in Box 4). This initiative would systematically look at the tools, techniques and standards to achieve this aim, through a governance lens that focuses on corruption fighting—an important driver of the recommendation.

The aim is to develop realistic good practice examples and guidance material useful to Task Team Leaders, client country project managers and communications practitioners. Some aspects to explore in this regard include how to quantify and incorporate qualitative corruption risk assessments at different stages of the project cycle through:

- standard risk assessments in project appraisals (plus tools to support that analysis);
- preparation of resettlement and livelihood plans and implementation arrangements (such as focusing on transparency to reduce corruption risk in the compensation payment process);
- EIAs, and particularly Environment Management Plans (EMPs), focusing on the risk of provision or non-provision, for example, of agreed river compensation flows in dams projects, this in terms of impacts on ecosystem services and traditional livelihoods;
- preparation of governance/anticorruption management plans as an explicit project component for implementation and operation phases with supporting communication strategies. In particular, this would aim to strengthen procurement plans in the implementation stages and maintenance procurement in operational phases, using the new anti-corruption tools; and
- improving project impact monitoring plans by incorporating feedback mechanisms to enable project beneficiaries to raise concerns about how well the project is working, the services they receive, and any governance issues they have.

From a Task Team Leader's perspective, this exercise needs to illustrate the skill mix required on missions—the expertise to draw on within the Bank or the consulting community. It should also reveal the time and budget implications for the project. From a communication practitioner's perspective, this exercise needs to show how the analysis informs the design communication assessments (what they must do that is new), how communication assistance (strategies, tools and techniques) can best be applied, as well as advise communication staff on what additional skills need to be developed.

Additionally it is important to have a clear idea if these tasks will be Bank or client executed, and, in the latter case, how they would fit institutionally in the client's project organization or the sponsoring Ministry. It is also worthwhile noting private sector practice. Corruption-fighting measures are normally part of corporate responsibility charters—usually under the executive responsible for corporate communications.

Implementing this initiative would likely involve a small steering committee with representation from appropriate groups in the World Bank and possibly international civil society observers (e.g., the Sustainable Development Network, Poverty Reduction and Economic Management (PREM) and Development communication) to provide directional guidance and to identify Task Leaders on four or five infrastructure projects to collaborate. Informal guidelines would seek to reflect good practice applicable to different infrastructure sectors.

Initiative 2: Instruments to Link National with Sector-level Reforms—Vertical Integration

The second initiative would have a similar aim but would be more limited in scope. It would focus on the linkages between national-level governance reform and sector-level reform, and specifically consider how communication processes and tools can enhance efforts to translate national policies into sector practice.

It would help lay the groundwork for involuntary communication standards and highlight features of two-way communication processes (and tools) proven to be most helpful in bringing sector policy-makers and infrastructure practitioners together around a common national platform for governance reform.

While this effort focuses on the water sector and dam planning and management practice, in particular, the initiative would seek to exploit synergy across sectors. The cross-sectoral look would be helpful, firstly, as this recognizes that progress in infrastructure reform in different sectors is often variable, due to the presence or absence of enabling conditions that are sector specific. Secondly, that in some sectors, such as the road or forest sector, many different countries have moved further than the water and other sectors in governance reform approaches and using communications tools, such as by introducing explicit Governance Improvement Plans and other innovations to combat corruption in infrastructure. Evidence suggests that many anti-corruption practices are transferable across sectors and there is interest in identifying such possibilities.[13] Further, it is possible to highlight replicable experiences of non-OECD countries, such as Botswana and Singapore, which have good national and sectoral integrity systems for anti-corruption reform.

Initiative 3: Engaging Media and Civil Society in Infrastructure Projects—Overcoming the "Pandora's Box" Fear

Many practitioners recognize that civil society and the media have a central role to play in the infrastructure development process in several ways. Even governments in the process

---

13. One example is Case Study 2 where anti-corruption elements were incorporated into a national road improvement project in Paraguay supported by the World Bank. Subsequently there has been interest and exploratory discussion at the national level on how the practices can be transferred to other sectors.

of reforming centrally planned economies, where advocacy NGOs and civil society have only recently been introduced, realize that without clear communication of the purpose of their reform agenda, they are not likely to win public buy-in and support for new policies.

The practical reality, however, is that project managers in client countries or the Ministry sponsoring an infrastructure project may be reluctant to engage with civil society—the media in particular. They may fear lighting up or giving space to controversy. The instinct also may be to control all information and events. In some cases conscious attempts to limit transparency to hide corrupt practices might be the underlying factor for resisting openness and engagement with stakeholders.

Good practice suggests that governance reforms related to infrastructure and services are always highly politicized. The biggest mistake for a project manager to make is not to engage with the media and civil society: assume that communication involves risks and thus adopt a no-action or minimalist approach to information flow. The second biggest mistake is to engage without a proper communication strategy, resources and professional support.[14]

This initiative, therefore, would focus on expanding the inventory of good practice examples to illustrate where strategic communication has led to an effective collaboration with media and civil society in infrastructure projects in different sectors and to a demonstrable improvement in the project. The pitfalls and problems of communicating reform in the infrastructure sector would be analyzed and preventative strategies provided. It would illustrate the motivations of the Task Team Leader and country client in engaging with media in the first place. The good practice inventory would include "turn around" examples, where the country client was reluctant to engage with media initially, but now pro-actively supports engagement with media and civil society.

Initiative 4: Bridging the Infrastructure and Communication Paradigms—Adding Value

As stated previously, part of the intellectual challenge in mainstreaming development communication is to bridge two different paradigms: infrastructure development and development communication. Demonstrating how communications link directly to the perceived needs of the infrastructure community, together with the illustration of the cost and value added from collaboration, would advance the argument for communication budgets and resources for projects.

The first aspect of this issue is to demonstrate the direct relevance of development communication in addressing concerns that politicians and infrastructure practitioners cite as their main challenges in pursuing infrastructure strategies. Different models exist to represent these concerns in a cross-section of developing countries. For example, the left column of Table 3 illustrates global mainstreaming concerns and trends in infrastructure that emerged from discussion with country clients and is cited in the World Bank's Infrastructure Report (World Bank 2005). The right column illustrates concerns from joint ADB and World Bank dialogue with politicians and infrastructure practitioners in Asia.

---

14. Adapted from Development communication, Adam Smith Institute, available at http://www.adamsmithinternational.com/pdf/ASI_Dev.pdf

Table 3. Global and Regional Mainstream Concerns in Infrastructure Development where Development Communication Can Add Value

Global Mainstreaming concerns and major trends in infrastructure	*Regional* Connecting East Asia: A new framework for infrastructure
■ Involving multiple-levels of government in infrastructure development and service provision ■ Unlocking private investment ■ Improving the quality of infrastructure ■ Ensuring response to priority development needs and balanced economic development ■ Inclusive development ■ Enhancing sustainability dimensions ■ Capturing development synergies ■ Addressing corruption	■ The center matters: infrastructure demands strong planning and coordination ■ Decentralization is important but raises a host of coordination challenges ■ Fiscal space for infrastructure is critical ■ "Subsidy" is not a dirty word: subsidies can be important but are always risky ■ Competition is hard to achieve in infra-structure but is best way to achieve accountability ■ Regulatory independence matters more in the long run than in the short run ■ Civil society has a key role in ensuring accountability in service provision ■ Infrastructure has to clean up its act, addressing corruption is a priority ■ The private sector will come back, if the right policies evolve ■ Public sector reform matters but be realistic ■ Local capital markets matter but are not a panacea ■ Infrastructure needs reliable and responsive development partners

Source: World Bank (2005); ADB, JBIC, and the World Bank (2005).

In effect, a strategic communication component would be added as a logical next step in responding to these concerns. Because this component builds on the work of infrastructure policy makers and practitioners, it would be an effective way to provide cogent communication advice while raising awareness of the potential of strategic communication among a key group of opinion formers. The exercise may go further to demonstrate why it is relevant and how best to use strategic communication to prepare the sector and project level initiatives that respond to their concerns (like the concerns noted in Table 3).

The second part of this initiative would mine information on existing projects to synthesize the hard evidence available on the costs savings realized from improving governance and linked to the communication role. While it may be generally accepted that communication is pivotal to mainstreaming good governance and anti-corruption measures, the more practical concern is how Task Team Leaders in MDBs and project sponsors actually weigh investments in communication (and governance improvement) against other calls on project budgets. Evidence suggests not enough weight is placed on these at the moment. In two projects cited earlier in this paper, the involvement of civil society and associated communication to introduce transparency in the procurement process resulted in nominal "savings" of US$64 million (a 8.5 percent cost reduction) and

US$14 million (an 18 percent cost reduction), respectively on projects in Mexico and Pakistan—significant amounts by any standards measured against the modest cost of the measures.

Initiative 5: Integrating Communication in the World Bank's Operational Policy Framework—A Future Orientation

The World Bank and other MDBs continuously update their operational policies defining support for infrastructure projects and sustainability dimensions. In the case of the World Bank, these include 10 environmental and social safeguard policies highlighted as the cornerstone of its support for sustainable poverty reduction and applicable to infrastructure projects.[15] Processes for updating operational policies take considerable time for consensus building.

Focusing on the operational policy framework for World Bank supported infrastructure projects, this initiative would have two orientations to systematically review future opportunities:

1. To map opportunities to imbed the role of communication in existing operational policies, and in particular the environmental and social safeguard policies, and
2. To identify concerns about how to imbed the role of communication in any future operational policy to deal explicitly with corruption and governance issues on infrastructure projects.

This would also be done to provide guidance notes for operational staff on the effective use of communication in meeting the current operational policies.

While the timing for any eventual operational policy on corruption in infrastructure projects may be argued, there is an opportunity to stimulate discussion. This has immediate relevance, for example, to the growing share of high-risk/high-reward infrastructure projects in the World Bank's portfolio, and the creation of the Sustainability Network after the recent merger of the Bank's central environment and social development departments into its infrastructure and energy units. It would support the MDB Common Framework Against Corruption, as agreed in Singapore in September 2006. MDBs committed to help member countries strengthen their capacity to combat corruption in cooperation with civil society, the private sector, media and other stakeholders.

---

15. There are 10 safeguard policies, comprising the Bank's policy on Environmental Assessment (EA) and policies on: Cultural Property; Disputed Areas; Forestry; Indigenous Peoples; International Waterways; Involuntary Resettlement; Natural Habitats; Pest Management; and Safety of Dams.http://web.world-bank.org/WBSITE/EXTERNAL/TOPICS/ENVIRONMENT/0,,contentMDK:20124313~menuPK:549278~pagePK:148956~piPK:216618~theSitePK:244381,00.html

A Growing Body of Evidence

There is growing evidence on the positive role and value added by strategic communication in improving governance and development outcomes in infrastructure projects in the power, water and transport sectors.

Experience in Relation to the World Congress on Communication for Development (WCCD) Conference Themes

Securing Political Will: The Prerequisite for Political Reform

Political will is essential to introduce and to drive governance improvements forward, in particular to establish the enabling legislation and regulatory frameworks for information access and for inclusive or informed decision-making appropriate to all levels of government.

Each case study shows that high-level political commitment to reform enabled the project to explicitly address governance issues in the project preparation phase. For example, when the new Administration assumed office in Paraguay in 2003, it focused the national development agenda on recovery from economic stagnation and fighting corruption in public institutions. The strong lead from central government enabled the road improvement project to adopt a "governance lens" in its design. It features a Governance Improvement Plan centered on corruption prevention, deterrence and detection that was developed in collaboration with road stakeholders.

In Sierra Leone, the post-war government recognized that corruption was a root cause of the 11-year rebel war that destroyed much of the country's physical and social infrastructure. After peace was restored, the Local Government Act (LGA-2004) defined a new

---

**Box 5: Communication Can Give Hard Evidence to Reinforce Political Support
         When it Counts**

The communication assessment in the project preparation phase of the Bumbuna Project flagged an important issue. Local communities fully expected to receive power services when the project became operational in 2–3 years. In fact, rural electrification was a much longer-term prospect. Unfilled expectations could threaten community cooperation on many different aspects of the project. The quantitative communication assessment was a factor in the decision to introduce non-power benefit sharing as a project component, where local communities were viewed as development partners.

---

development paradigm built upon the principles of transparency, inclusion, accountability and sustainability. It essentially devolved decision-making from central Ministries to more accountable locally elected councils. The political drive behind this governance reform enabled the Bumbuna project team to work with local Councils and communities directly to build community-driven development approaches into the environment and social management components of the project and to introduce non-power local benefit sharing arrangements, which in previous times would have been difficult if not impossible to consider.

Similarly, in post-apartheid South Africa, the political will behind legislation for participatory planning and public consultation in all water management decisions at local, provincial and national levels empowered public debate on Berg Water Supply Project. The outcome of the debate was a decision to balance new investment in supply infrastructure with water demand management.

In Mexico, political will enabled the Federal Electricity Commission (*Comision Federal de Electricidad*—CFE) to work with civil society actors to introduce transparency in the public procurement processes.

In each of these four cases, communication played a role in creating consensus for political decisions at the project level when it counted. As Box 5 shows, the communication assessment on the Bumbuna project provided hard evidence to give central government the confidence to approve local benefit-sharing arrangements also supported by local government. These measures not only enhance poverty alleviation in the poorest region of the country, but also paved the way to work effectively with host communities as partners on the longer-term measures important to the sustainability of the project, which included land-use management changes as part of watershed management.

Strengthening Voice and Accountability: The Endgame of Communication for Development

In infrastructure development, the aim is to give voice to all stakeholders in the selection, development and management of infrastructure projects where not only consensus, but also improvements in the quality of infrastructure projects are sought. This means giving voice to strengthen accountability at all levels of government and with project partners to honor commitments and agreements and to address corruption at all stages of the project cycle. It also means reaching out to stakeholders who are not vocal but have much to contribute to the quality of projects and to monitoring the impacts.

Box 6: Communication Can Leverage Large Financial Returns through Accountability

---

For the El Cajon Hydropower project the transparency monitoring of the bid award process led by *Transparencia Mexicana's* was comparatively inexpensive. The successful consortium bid was US$64 million under the original cost estimate of US$840 million, prepared based on historical bidding trends. Whether this "savings" can be attributed transparency alone may be argued. The voice of civil society, however, can clearly leverage significant returns.

In Paraguay, road stakeholders were asked to set out and to discuss collectively their respective views on how the Governance Improvement Plan could be carried forward. The Government saw how expanding the voice of civil society in public policy and in control of public expenditures was central to restoring confidence in public institutions. A social impact monitoring plan was included in the project that will enable beneficiaries and civil society to provide feedback on the project impacts and governance concerns.

In Sierra Leone, measures such as establishing a community radio station were among the many steps to give voice to local communities on project issues that concerned them. Similarly, in the debate on water supply infrastructure in Cape Town, Public Consultation Guidelines issued by the Department of Water Affairs and Forestry (DWAF) offered guidance on steps to ensure all stakeholders had a voice in the decision process. Many media channels were also present to represent stakeholder views in Cape Town.

As Box 6 illustrates, civil society's perspective on the bid process for the El Cajon Hydropower project yielded a significant dividend for the *Comision Federal de Electricidad* (CFE). The "social witness" (*testigo social*) report was placed on *Transparencia Mexicana's* website for all stakeholders to view, including the bidding companies. The report was also written with setting standards in mind.

Making Public Institutions Transparent: The Cornerstone of an Open Society

In infrastructure development, transparency primarily means helping public institutions that sponsor infrastructure projects to apply the approved policies for democratization of the development process. This involves ensuring the mechanisms are in place for information access, coordination with other agencies and structured processes for consultations with stakeholders, as well as openness in public financial management that is essential to fight grand and petty corruption.

The road maintenance project in Paraguay sought to use tools appropriate to a weak governance setting. First, it directly focused on the budget allocation question and introduced a monitoring system to generate different categories of "alerts," the most serious of which prompted independent investigations. In addition to the road social contracts, the project sought to introduce inter-institutional relationship agreements where roles could be confirmed.

In Sierra Leone, the lack of transparency in line ministries was addressed largely by devolving many of the development decisions on medium- and small-scale infrastructure to the elected District Councils where a more open and transparent approach was actually feasible. For the Bumbuna project, a Trust with a multi-stakeholder governing board will

> ### Box 7: Communication Reinforces Transparency in Public Institutions
>
> The Water Services Act (1997) in South Africa required each public utility to prepare a Municipal Water Service Development Plan (WSDP) in two years. WSDP incorporated new water demand projections, identified infrastructure requirements, provided a water balance, and reviewed the environmental management issues associated with current and future water service provision.
>
> Each utility was required to establish a communication strategy and public hearing process to prepare a draft WSDP.

be introduced to manage local investments that derive from benefit sharing financing mechanisms, allocating resources through a grant-based application procedure that is open and transparent at all steps and monitored by civil society.

In South Africa, the Municipal Water Services Act (1997) required all water supply utilities to conduct infrastructure planning and investment transparently. Part of the political motivation was to introduce greater equity in water supply tariffs and services.

As Box 7 shows, an immediate effect of increasing transparency of public institutions is the growing need for communication processes, not only to enable the water utilities to engage with stakeholders on infrastructure choice, but also to establish public communication capacities required to explain and conduct public debate on difficult tariff reforms essential to ensure sustainable infrastructure services.

Fighting Corruption: Beyond Technocratic Solutions

In infrastructure development, fighting corruption means taking action on a number of fronts simultaneously. Moving beyond technocratic solutions also means challenging the basic cultural norms that tolerate corruption on infrastructure projects. Experience suggests this requires wider engagement with institutions outside line ministries and agencies, such as parliament, civil society, non-governmental organizations, the media and local communities, to complement ongoing work with government institutions.

In the road maintenance project in Paraguay, the Road Social Contracts introduced in the Governance Improvement Plan were viewed as central to longer-term attitudinal changes. In the Sierra Leone, the Bumbuna project places local communities who participate in benefit sharing arrangements at the forefront of efforts to introduce social accountability measures at the grass roots level, in order to keep local corruption at bay. The public debate on the Berg Municipal Water Supply Project helped to avoid the perception of undue political influence on the decision-making processes and to provide legitimacy for the decisions

> ### Box 8: Communication Facilitates Processes of Social Change and Reform
>
> On the road improvement project in Paraguay, the project sponsor, the Ministry of Public Works and Communication (MOPC) will enter into Road Social Contracts with representatives of the road users, the contractors, local governments and congressmen. These social contracts will be developed over a number of meetings and workshops, on a multilateral and bilateral basis with the stakeholders. They will capture commitments of all stakeholders to fight corruption with changes in practices and behaviour.

Box 9: Communication May Encompass Capacity Building for Media Roles in Infrastructure

---

The Bumbuna project signed an agreement with the "Information, Education and Communication Unit" of the National Commission for Social Action (NACSA), to provide technical assistance and quality control for the Bumbuna Hydro communication activities.

An important communication task was to maintain direct relationships and dialogue with journalists in Sierra Leone, to provide material they could use to produce articles and accurate news reports (e.g., updated press kits with informational material, pictures, interviews—written and on tape) and to support media visits to the site.

---

taken, especially since many detractors thought that undue influence of larger institutions was the main factor driving proposals for infrastructure projects. It also promoted the notion that public dialogue before such decisions is the norm, not the exception.

In each of the four cases, communication processes helped to provide a platform for building consensus on corruption fighting and long-term behavior shifts. As Box 8 illustrates, communication processes are important to facilitate the stakeholders work toward a negotiated outcome on the Road Social Contract—part of Paraguay's approach to improve governance and fight corruption.

Building Media Systems: Enabling an Effective Fourth Estate

In infrastructure development, building an effective fourth estate primarily means the project sponsor and partners must support media with timely access to information about the project. All project partners, including project managers and decision-makers in government, must operate within the spirit and intent of applicable laws on information access. It also means working proactively with the different media and enabling them to interact with stakeholders as part of a comprehensive communication strategy.

While media training and capacity building support may be outside the scope of some infrastructure projects, certainly this could be a strategic initiative in sector strengthening projects. Given the many roles of media in governance and fighting corruption, particularly in countries with very low levels of media capacity, helping to build the fourth estate would help to increase transparency and to facilitate infrastructure development.

The road maintenance project in Paraguay views the role of media in terms of disseminating project information and increasing transparency and accountability throughout its cycle. In South Africa, the media systems that evolved after apartheid now reflect deeply the principles of inclusiveness. There was extensive media coverage of the Berg Project to inform the public of ongoing events and how they might choose to interact with the decision-making process. In the end, this enabled the Minister to inform Parliament when sufficient consensus was reached.

In the Bumbuna project, interaction with the media was an important part of the project preparation. The communication plan provides for regular interaction with journalists in the print and electronic media.

As Box 9 shows, it was important to work with media to build capacity not only for the Bumbuna Project needs, but also to position the media to play a constructive role informing public debate on the future hydropower development in Sierra Leone.

Case Studies

Case Study 1. Paraguay: Road Maintenance Project[16]

This infrastructure project demonstrates how anti-corruption elements were incorporated into a national road improvement project supported by the World Bank. A Governance Improvement Plan and Road Social Contracts were instruments used to capture the measures stakeholders agreed upon for corruption prevention, deterrence and detection, and to ensure public expenditure is sustainably balanced between road expansion and road maintenance. A social impact monitoring plan will enable beneficiaries and civil society to provide feedback on the project impacts.

The Context. When the new Administration assumed national office in Paraguay in 2003, it committed to focus the country's development agenda on recovery from economic stagnation and on fighting corruption. Expanding the participation of civil society in public policy formulation and controlling public expenditures was viewed by the Administration to be an important step, new for Paraguay, to restore confidence in public institutions and to move the anti-corruption effort forward.

Improvements in road infrastructure were key to advancing the country's economic performance and to realizing the government's strategy to shift the economy to agro-industry and diversified exports. Most indicators showed that Paraguay had fallen well behind neighboring countries in terms of road transport performance and competitiveness. In 2004, road transport accounted for 10 percent of all public expenditures but suffered

---

16. See the Project Appraisal Document http://web.worldbank.org/external/projects/main?page PK=64283627&piPK=73230&theSitePK=342833&menuPK=342867&Projectid=P082026

from endemic corruption. Paraguay ranks next to the bottom in the Transparency International's (TI) corruption perception index (CPI) for all countries.

Thus when Paraguay approached the World Bank in 2004 to support its program to improve its network of priority and secondary roads (mostly unpaved) and road access for the poorest and most excluded rural communities, the links between the sustainability of road investment and the governance environment to modernize road administration and to contain corruption were on the agenda.

The Measures Adopted. The World Bank team and Ministry of Public Works and Communication (MOPC) involved the key stakeholders in a two-year collaborative process to develop the project parameters, which included a governance diagnostics exercise. While defining anti-corruption measures was part of the discussion, one aspect that took time was to establish consensus on a sustainable road management strategy to balance between infrastructure expansion and maintenance expenditures. Rebalancing investment between road expansion and maintenance was key to moving to a sustainable approach in the sector, but this also called for a new alignment of stakeholder interests.

What emerged as a central feature of the project was an Improved Governance Action Plan. The World Bank's Department of Institutional Integrity provided technical input on global practices. This Plan establishes three guiding themes for the physical components of the project: (a) *performance enhancement,* through monitoring targets whose attainment would indicate success; (b) *accountability,* through planning and programming all interventions on the basis of objective and quantifiable criteria; and (c) *participation and transparency,* through mechanisms that allow stakeholders to influence and share control over the decision-making.

Enhanced supervision and monitoring will be triggered by biannual reports showing indicators of potential inefficiencies or "alerts" (such as when the number of firms participating in bids drop below three). If the indicators of potential fraud or "red flags" (such as improper communication with contractors) occur during enhanced supervision, then the team reports its findings to the Department of Institutional Integrity (INT). If the gravity of the flags is deemed high, INT will investigate.

Another innovative instrument in the governance plan was a Road Social Contract designed to clarify and capture the stakeholder commitments. These will be co-signed by the MOPC and representatives of the road users, contractors, local governments and congressmen during the implementation phase of the project. The contract will reflect the agreed roles that emerge from dialogue processes. They symbolize not only MOPC's adherence to the Road Strategy, but also the contributions of each stakeholder towards the strategy, as well as roles and behaviors of each party that contribute implicitly to fighting corruption and to enhancing the governance environment. The expectation is that the Social Contracts will be followed up with bilateral agreements between the MOPC and the parties. Figure 3 shows an example of public information material prepared by one participating department in the national road improvement project.

Communication was the organizing principle of the project's Social Participation Framework (EPS) that had participation, communication and transparency components aimed at all social actors, the public and beneficiaries. A feature in the EPS design was social analysis. This assessed how to target the investments in improving road access in remote rural areas to maximize poverty alleviation. It developed a social impact monitoring plan

Figure 3. Public Promotion for the National Road Rehabilitation Project, Paraguay

that will allow the project beneficiary communities to provide feedback on how well the services are improving and to express any governance concerns.

The Value Added by Communication. Clearly, the lead taken by the national government to improve transparency and governance enabled the project to be designed through a governance lens, as noted in the Project Appraisal. Communication and social assessments were key to reaching consensus among stakeholders on how the sustainability and anti-corruption aims would be addressed. Many meetings and workshops were held to disseminate and discuss international good practice in improving governance with civil society participating. While it is too early to assess the impact of the measures agreed, what is evident is the tone set by the dialogue signaled that corruption is a social cancer holding back Paraguay's socio-economic progress and could no longer be tolerated in the road sector.

Consensus on the content of 4 Road Social Contracts will be established in a further round of meetings and workshops during the implementation phase. A structured communication process will ensure transparent agreements in which the media and civil society will also play an important monitoring role, such as ensuring public notice of tender calls and bid evaluation criteria and publishing information on awarded procurement contracts. Figure 4 shows the signing of a road social contract by a participating department. This was an important element of the Governance Improvement Plan to help clarify roles and commitments of stakeholders in the project activities and anti-corruption measures.

Traditional communication arrangements are also at the core of and central to the success of the transparency and accountability components of the Social Participation Framework. Here the system will allow for timely flow of reliable information accessible to all social actors according to their needs and cultural characteristics through vehicles such as websites, written press, radio, informative bulletins and newsletters, among others. The beneficiary feedback from the social impact monitoring plan will also be in the public domain.

Figure 4. Signing Ceremony for a Road Social Contract *(contrato social via)* in Paraguay

Case Study 2. Sierra Leone: The 50 MW Completion of the Bumbuna Hydroelectric Project

This case demonstrates the effective integration of strategic communication in the preparation of a hydropower completion project in a post-war reconstruction setting. It conceives of communication as facilitating consensus in the distribution of the project benefits and enabling a grass-roots voice in developing the environment and social management components of the project. The communication assessment was also instrumental in identifying social conflicts among project-affected groups that could have impeded project implementation, or limited community participation in crucial activities designed to raise local incomes and to ensure the project's environmental sustainability. This enabled consensus to be established on remedial measures and reflect these in the project design. Social accountability approaches using civil society actors will be an important part of transparency in local expenditures to address worries about opportunities for local corruption.

The Context. When Sierra Leone asked the international community for help to complete the 50 MW Completion of Bumbuna Hydroelectric Project (BHP) in 2003, the country was just emerging from an 11-year rebel war. The conflict had displaced almost half of the country's 5.8 million people and left much of its physical and social infrastructure destroyed. After the war officially ended and general elections were held (mid-2002), completion of the BHP to restore power supply in the county was a post-war priority. The Bumbuna project in fact was 80 percent complete when it was abandoned in 1997 due to the escalating conflict. It had long been symbolic of future prosperity for Sierra Leone, as a means to reduce reliance on costly imported oil, provide a reliable power supply and start electrification of the country.

Just as the two-year project preparation tasks were getting under way, the new government introduced legislation that fundamentally changed the country's governance

Figure 5. View of the Morning Glory Spillway of the Bumbuna Hydroelectric Project, Sierra Leone

system. The Local Government Act (LGA-2004) defined a new governance paradigm that, in recognition of the causes of civil war, built upon the principles of transparency, inclusion, accountability and sustainability. It provided for a new assignment of functional responsibilities across national, provincial and local levels of government that essentially reactivated local government institutions and devolved decision-making on local infrastructure development and public service delivery to local councils to be elected. Political space was also maintained for the traditional governance systems.

In the power sector, private sector participation was to be introduced to address the legacy of under resourcing, under performance and perceived corruption in the sector. The BHP itself was to be pursued as a public-private project, the first in the country. Sierra Leone also ranked near the bottom of the Transparency International's (TI) corruption perception index (CPI) for all countries.

The Measures Adopted. The initial measure was to ensure strategic communication was an integral part of the up-front project preparation. Provision was made for a World Bank communications professional and an experienced communications practitioner to be part of the project preparation team. In parallel, an enlightened management team on the government side established a communications unit with full-time communications staff. The initial work was diagnostic in nature and included three main tasks:

- *Communication assessment:* strategically scans for risks of controversy and other threats to the project's successful completion and otherwise ensures the project development objectives were well identified, understood and agreed to by stakeholders. Techniques employed included in-depth interviews and consultations with politicians, government and civil society and direct sampling of the views of traditional leaders and people at the project site.

■ *Media environment assessment:* assesses media capacities in Sierra Leone, establishes how communications professionals perceived the project and how media at the national and local levels could best contribute to the communication strategy. This included an assessment of local NGOs to evaluate their capacity to act partners in communication activities.

■ *Public opinion research:* assesses the overall public perception of the project, carried out by an independent media consultant.

The project communication strategy founded on two-way communication principles was prepared after the diagnostics work. This strategy was presented to the multi-agency technical committee responsible for overseeing all aspects of the project implementation, and indeed, the committee was keen to understand and comment on the strategy. The technical committee also reported to a cabinet-level committee led by the Vice-President of Sierra Leone.

The communications team launched the approved communication process at national levels and with the communities directly affected by the project. Actions to engage national stakeholders included national radio talk shows, information on TV and in print media. A web site was prepared for international stakeholders to monitor the project preparation activities—this in addition to the normal disclosure requirements of the World Bank. Communications structures put in place at the project site included a radio station to enable community-led discussion programs to take place through all stages of project implementation, in addition to "town criers", theatre troops and information centers strategically located in the impact area.

The communications unit was an integral part of dialogue to achieve consensus with local communities on the social and environment management components of the project. This necessitated addressing concerns people had about resettlement and livelihood restoration (along the transmission line and Bumbuna reservoir area). Additionally the dialogue introduced benefit sharing arrangements for communities in the project area and the type of initiatives they preferred, as an alternative to local power services that would not be feasible in the near-term due to costs. Figure 6 shows the public consultation held in the Bumbuna Village during the official launch of the Bumbuna Community Radio, Radio Numbara FM 102.5.

The Value Added by Communication. In 2003 the project was seen as largely "benign," with limited adverse social and environmental impacts. It was viewed as enjoying public support with manageable reputation and project risks, as the main construction risk was already absorbed. The communication analysis revealed, however, that since 1997, misinformation, rumors and mistrust had spread among various groups of stakeholders nationwide, including communities in the project area. Even high-ranking government officials had misperceptions or little information about the project status.

At the center of public and local community concern was widespread mistrust of "corrupt politicians"—based on past practice. Why would anything be different this time? Moreover, it emerged that tribal tensions existed in the project area that could jeopardize the project's cooperation with communities, particularly with regard to resettlement activities, community-managed land use and biodiversity conservation measures. These measures were part of the sustainability of the project performance and catchment management to control soil erosion

Figure 6. Launch of Radio Numbara FM 102.5 at Bumbuna Village, Sierra Leone

and sedimentation that also required strong inter-community cooperation. The risk was disagreements over project issues would aggravate local tensions in the post-war situation.

Avoidance of unfilled expectations emerged as another important concern. As the communication assessments revealed, most local communities thought they would receive power services when the project became operational in two to three years time when, in fact, rural electrification was a much longer-term proposition. The project team was thus able to introduce non-power benefit sharing arrangements (funded by local project revenue and carbon financing) and to integrate community-driven development approaches in the environment and social management mechanisms. Political consensus on this approach was possible as the communication work provided hard evidence of the need to address the local concerns through benefit-sharing arrangements. Figure 7 shows the Radio Numbara Community Radio producers at work, preparing the afternoon local news program.

Dealing with legacy compensation issues was an additional sensitive element. In the 1990's compensation was not paid to people at the dam site and to people moved for the transmission towers along the 200 km of transmission right-of-way. People feared that the compensation they were entitled to and promised would be stolen. The communication team helped the Ministry tackle these issues and maintain confidence in the agreed process.

Two further contributions were a by-product of capacity strengthening to implement the project communication strategy. First, the activities contributed to capacity building of media stakeholders. While this was important for the project, it was also a vital step in positioning the media to play a constructive role informing public debate on the future hydropower development in Sierra Leone. Secondly, a successful Bumbuna project—one not perceived to be riddled with corruption (in the new governance context)—was of vital importance to build public confidence in the government's overall strategy of promoting private sector participation in infrastructure development in all sectors.

Figure 7. Radio Numbara FM 102.5 "on air" (Sierra Leone)

Case Study 3. South Africa: Berg Municipal Water Supply Project

This case demonstrates the importance of public communication capacity for water utilities investment in infrastructure and for management of reforms in water supply services to improve equity in services access. It shows how a combination of legislative reform and new guidelines for public consultation made the public institutions involved more transparent and accountable. These steps empowered public debate to reach a decision on water supply infrastructure for Cape Town, which was controversial at the time, while firmly placing demand-side management on the agenda. This promoted a sustainable supply-demand balance that met with wider public acceptance (World Bank 2003b).

The Context. In 1998, the Cape Metropolitan Council (CMC, later to become the CCT) proposed building the Skuifraam dam to augment municipal water supply and provide security against drought. The CMC sought the approval of the national government that would co-finance any project. The Berg River is one of the last free flowing rivers in the region. A coalition of environmental communities, water recreation interests and proponents of demand-side management opposed the project.

The Skuifraam proposal came just after completion of a major transformation of legislation governing water management policies and practices in South Africa—now regarded as among the most progressive in the world. For example, the National Water Act (1998) introduced legal requirements for environmental reserves in the regulation of river flows. Relevant to the Skuifraam question, the Water Services Act (1997) required municipalities to openly and transparently assess alternatives before proposing new dams. New legislation introduced in the water resources and environment management fields reinforced participatory planning and public consultation in all major water management decisions taken at local, provincial and national levels.

While the debate was proceeding in 2000, the Department of Water Affairs and Forestry (DWAF) issued new national guidelines for public consultations on water resource projects. At this time also, water use restrictions were first imposed by the CCT on municipal water users and the agricultural sector (1999–2000) due to drought and resulting water scarcity.

The Measures Adopted. After the former CMC requested national approval for Berg project, the Minister responsible advised Parliament that any decision to augment municipal water supply in Cape Town would be predicated on three factors: (1) a review of the demand projections; (2) a clear indication of the commitment of the Cape Town and the Transitional Local Councils and District Councils to demand management; and (3) provision of better technical information on the potential of demand management and the budgetary needs. In response, the CCT, working with the media, immediately strengthened its water demand management activities by mounting awareness and information programs. Water tariffs were restructured, and bans and restrictions were introduced on water uses, such as lawn watering. While acknowledging progress, the NGO constituency criticized these measures as wholly inadequate.

An extensive program of studies, consultations with the special interest groups and public hearings on the Berg Project were organized around the three separate decision-making processes. These processes involved: (1) preparation of the new Municipal-level Water Service Development Plan (WSPD) led by the CMC, that was required in a two-year timeframe; (2) the Berg WMA planning process, a larger water resources management planning area in which Cape Town was situated, led by the DWAF; and (3) the EIA process for the Skuifraam dam led by the Environment Affairs Ministry.

After each of the processes was completed, the Minister for Water Affairs eventually gave approval in principle to proceed with the Berg project in 2001. It was announced that the project would go hand-in-hand with a more aggressive water management program. After subsequent Parliamentary sub-committee debate, in May 2002, the Cabinet authorized the Berg Water Project. Figure 8 shows the construction of the intake of the Berg (Skuifraam

Figure 8. Construction of the Berg Water Supply Dam (Photo Courtesy of Water Wheel)

Dam). The first supply of water to the Cape Town area from the scheme is expected to begin by the end of 2007. The dam wall, including its foundation, will be 70 metres high and 990 metres long. It will be the highest concrete-faced, rock-filled dam in South Africa.

The Value Added by Communication. The Berg decision process, in effect, became a first major test of the workings of the new legislation and public consultation framework in the Western Cape Province. The 9 governance reforms that centered on participatory decision-making triggered a much wider public debate on water management policy. This prompted calls for a fundamental rethinking of the role of infrastructure and balancing demand and supply management as a sustainable approach.

This case also shows the complexity of development communication at the sector level. Parallel communication processes were required in all three decision-making processes that had a bearing on the ultimate infrastructure choices. The presence of legislation and guidelines that implicitly provided common "rules" for government ministries and agencies to engage stakeholders and public consultation, nevertheless, meant that each process adopted the same principles of openness, transparency and well-advertised mechanisms for public voice.

The media played a key role presenting the different points of view to the public. This was done through articles and reporting on the various meetings in which officials convened with stakeholders individually and together, as the studies to inform the debate became available. This openness ultimately gave the Minister confidence to advise Parliament when sufficient consensus was reached and the no-decision outcome was avoided. Figure 9 shows a group of children who were interviewed by the project team as part of the social monitoring process. The children were asked to draw pictures depicting their interpretation of the project. The drawings were used to gauge the impact of the project on their lives as well as their perceptions of the project.

Due to the combination of factors (for example, pressure from the media, mechanisms to allow space in the debate for diverse views, and the presence of enabling legislation) a

Figure 9. A Workshop to Assess Children's Perceptions of the Berg Water Project (Photo Courtesy of Siobhan McCarthy)

better balance between new supply and demand management was struck. Despite some remaining polarized views, it was widely regarded as a more sustainable outcome than the original thinking of the Cape Metropolitan Council.

Case Study 4. Mexico: The 750 MW El Cajon Hydropower Project

This case demonstrates the value of independent verification and review of contract bid and contractor selection processes for hydropower projects, together with the value of increased civil society participation in monitoring the contract award process. It illustrates techniques suitable to scale-up across the power sector and replicate in public procurement processes in other infrastructure sectors. The modest investment in transparency contributed significantly to a US$64 million difference (8.5 percent lower) successful bid than the original cost estimate.

The Context. Energy reform and modernization of the power industry is highly politicized in Mexico. Since the 1960's the electricity sector has been reserved for the State. Law limits private participation in generation activities. Funds to increase the country's generation capacity therefore have to come from the federal budget and transparency in public expenditure is most important.

Between 2001 and March 2005, *Transparencia Mexicana* completed 15 Integrity Pacts (IPs) working with various government agencies in Mexico and had another 12 ongoing (see Box 3 for a description of IPs). While following the same principles as the IP model developed by Transparency International (TI), the Mexican IP introduced an additional feature to increase citizen participation in the contracting award process. This employed a "social witness or *testigo social*" to oversee the contracting process and to communicate the results to the rest of civil society and the public. The social witness selected by *Transparencia Mexicana* must be an independent and respected technical expert in the field.

At the request of the relevant contracting agencies, *Transparencia Mexicana* (TI-Mexico) arranged for the hiring of social witnesses for projects in the water sector, such as the 750 MW El Cajon hydroelectric project under the responsibility of the Federal Electricity Commission (*Comision Federal de Electricidad*, CFE) and the operation of a Wastewater Treatment Plant under the responsibility of the Municipality of Saltillo. Figure 10 shows the location of the project in south-western Mexico.

The Measures Adopted. The following outlines the steps undertaken by TI-Mexico in relation to its involvement in the contracting and procurement process for the El Cajon hydroelectric project over the period August 2002 to June 2003. The basic features of the approach were the following:

- The designation of a social witness to monitor the process by TI-Mexico.
- As a condition for competing for the project, each bidder was required to make a unilateral Declaration of Integrity, signed by the highest level official of the bidding consortia. Similar declarations were submitted by CFE officials and by all Government officials involved in the bidding process.

Figure 10. Location of the El Cajon Hydroelectric

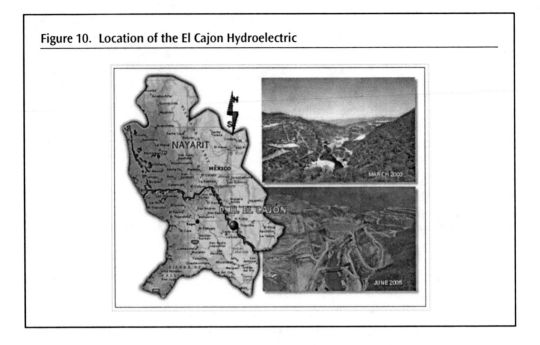

- Based on interviews with each prospective bidder, TI-Mexico concluded that the bidders were most concerned about the fairness of the evaluation process.
- Of the 30 prospective bidders who purchased the bidding documents (covering the civil and electromechanical aspects of the project), 21 did not submit proposals. Of the remaining entities, ten split into three consortia that submitted proposals. These proposals were evaluated in terms of technical acceptability.
- A contract of US$748 million equivalent was then awarded to the lowest evaluated bid of a consortium comprising *Constructora internacional de Infraestructura, Promotora e Invesora Adisa, Ingenieros Civiles Asociados, La Peninsular Compania Constructora and Energomacexport-Power Machine*. The successful bid was 8.5 percent lower than the original project cost estimate prepared by the CEF.

During the bidding process, TI-Mexico received one complaint about an alleged irregularity in the bidding process, which alleged CFE had provided confidential information to one bidder five months before the start of the bidding process. TI requested a meeting with the complainant but received no response. In response to a request for its reaction to the complaint allegation, CFE informed TI-Mexico that it had posted information on the Internet months ahead of the tender, requesting feedback on the project from all interested stakeholders. None of the bidders complained about the qualification criteria or about the legal framework of the contracting process. According to TI-Mexico, there were no unresolved complaints in relation to the project. Figure 11 shows the construction of the El Cajon dam and power house as of January 2007.

At the conclusion of his involvement in the project, the social witness prepared a report, which was posted on TI-Mexico's webpage. The witness report covered the following areas: observations and recommendations on the contracting process; a review of